THE MONARCHS

Cover art used with permission of the artist, Heide Hinrichs.

First Edition, January 2013

Library of Congress Cataloging-in-Publication Data
Noel, Melanie 1968-
    THE MONARCHS
    poems by Melanie Noel
    ISBN 978-0-9840285-4-2   (Paperback)

Stockport **Flats** 2013

1120 East Martin Luther King Jr. Street   Ithaca, NY 14850   (607) 272-1630

www.stockportflats.org

THE MONARCHS

Melanie Noel

CONTENTS

NURSING HOME SUBLIME

SHARIRA

for Martha Nell and Zula Pearl

TRACT

Mourning doves eclipse the sun with the insectual sigh of their flying.

The *port of morrow* is faint and various.

Barley in the burial hall.

Funeral of the lock.

Love will not always love you, someone   a pop song said

One definition of canal is *any of various faint narrow markings held to exist on the planet Mars.*

*

There is a green moonlight the animist forgives

forgiving Abraham.   The heart-shaped leaf does not make

a heart-shaped shadow.

In Iowa the roots are starving.   Decorous yellow fast.

In the chalk fields of Épernay the grapes suckle from the guarded earth

and in you Erie, a feast of ships and barley   *   vary me into your boundary

Sun that is a soldier's memory

Invisibly and peacefully drift on tiny feet　　　　　(it is getting away)

The wet paper of the sky —

Water drawls into ceiling lamps.

The apocalypse is not coming.

*

Questions faint and various as eggs　　　Invisible in the sunglint　cats test the ice.

We too this film that forgettable becomes

Docent, Erie.

The world is so beautiful. The branches here so brutalized.

*

Faint various

Goldfinch wick

the Flickrd Flower.

THE MONARCHS

TANGO OF THE TIRED SUN

Come away from the smoldering grave

              The lemon emigrants are erasing and erasing the woods

             Even the fox, after

    the lashes of the sun

THE LION ANT

I had seen your pelt in the transparent woods: unclean

but gleaming. Plainspoken the birds and the yellow earth.

*

Black thousand:

Industrial sun:

Ball bearing of the hunt:

Heart, hidden.

*

I had seen your pelt in the woods and nothing else.

But then my eye did hear

                        the colony

                ecliptic

bowed forepaws marching

                as if in dark honey.

INTERSTATE

Every other egg is a gambling saint and turns away

gold and clutching   in a perfume

of cocoa and rust   She spills from the yellow dress naming

chiffon must   pitch green

in an aura of gardenia

and eaglet

edged in dark red   she is

spilling from the yellow dress   in an avalanche

of light light

KORA, KORAI

Bee cave   maiden bees   pour in through the eyes   spur the memorized

        Grief   spring Fruit *Euphoria longana*   leak the dull water

Heart, open onto the tongue
                        (cardinal who guards the

        Threshold   turning back

          Pour in through the eyes   hum surgical, hum

AUTOBIOGRAPHY

A blackbird burrows in the gold dust. Shore dweller, cast your spell upon yourself.
Be asleep again
in the cashmere dawn, hypnagogic. Not gone.

Things that explode and make unpleasant sounds: Grenades. Lightning, especially in the afternoon,
when trying to get things done, and especially when it strikes metal. At night it is more beautiful.

Insects that make one tense: Gnats, when there are many. Ladybugs. Beetles, when they are on their
backs.

Shape flow and transformation habit. I was nine days old. _____
_____
_____. And that's how I learned to be alone, my stupid glass eye in my pocket.
I wandered in the courtyard of miracles, tripping over dead horses. They couldn't see me either.
The doctor turned his body to the sink and kept turning.

Covetable positions: The thief, if he is successful. The sage.

California is a beautiful state. I was conceived there in the summer of love. I was conceived by
virgins under a tree draped with monarchs. It is almost too much.

Things that make you want to walk away: The labor of violence. The labor of love. The state flowers and the flower states. My scythe of love. My state of states.

Things which sound like other things: Garbage trucks like dinosaurs. Trains like earthquakes. This is also a feeling. A baby's cry and an airplane also sometimes sound alike.

In Grunewald the trees are the tails of dead rats. One can hear the trains which no longer come.

The volcano also holds trees upon it, dead but rooted.

The doctor turns his eyes and his body and makes tiny lectures from his cavities while the nobleman listens red-eyed for rhymes. The heart turns away counting. Maybe the doctor is thinking as he turns away *I must dominate reality.* Maybe he recalls a madness he may adopt.

Prior to speech: No one is coming. You are quiet in your box and no one comes. You close the door with your hands of dough and deafness and it will not close. This was just a way to keep the keeping away away. You turn. There is the sound of television and monarchs. Laughter that is yellow and black.

My neighbor pets the dying bees as they ride into winter on dead stems.

The nuts are buried shallowly. The war sees to itself.

It thinks of you when you aren't there.

(stilts and limbs of the sea)

Things people say and shouldn't: It's just that. I'm sorry. I'm lost. I won. We regret to inform you.
I'm sorry. I am old. It is here I had her. Do you want me? So.

It rains along the walls and the walls surrender. Hello walls. Hello rain. *Salutations.*
They are speechless. They are shy. It is too much. There are earworms in the aperture.

Dark page. Bright distance.

The doctor turns like a country song. It takes a long time. It is as if he is *sleepwalking through history.*

The Smell of the Air is Red

Base & summit   valley and tail

like the original mouth of the year you were born

pale with shame and tanks

the cursive desire of sunlight

pressing on an unsure horizon.

Truths which could be lies: No one will come. No one is coming.

Memory, keep your eyes to the front. Tails behind you and roots underground. Make marks. The egg
is overtaken. The monarchs blink back dusk.

Things that cause doubt: Phone calls from creditors. Absence. His wandering eye.

Desire deforms us. We are centipedes in the banana trees. For purchase the catastrophic light.

Things which could be said to incite courage: As kale is strong are we! Oblivion River Never!

The bed tries to remember how we stayed in it reading to each other; how you put an onion
in my hand and I fainted. Instead it recalls the bugs circulating along the wall. It hears the trains.

Things the interviewer asked the Italian secretary: But you've some aim? A hope?

(A machine gun? Birds?)

Things she answered: It was a sop to my conscience. I wanted to come up against reality. I wanted
to get rid of alibis. I wanted to live on my own terms. I wanted to be with someone — without
ghosts. I wanted to die to get out of myself.

Pillar of mirrors pillar of ancestors   the ocean in my suitcase adrift   a gaze   palliative ocean egg-shaped doorknob on the gates of hell

Things that fly: Owls. Astronauts. Angels.
Maple seeds.

Monarch, do you see the droning angels? Step out of your lace.

STRANGEL MINE

Microphone of dead pine   canary in the lightwell   salt on the rind

aviary eyelet.

Volcano opens the earth rain

opens the clouds sunflower opens the ground   *The stars*

withdraw from the sky.

The deed is airless and weightless.

(The horse a sudden orchid)

Atlas of Mnemosyne,

The shine   eyelet & starling

Microphone

microphone   lightwell

WARM EARTH

Not the sun dance   unless   hooked to the sun

Orange   out of bloom   bright   shrugging Other the

      fanning mock orange   ! . . . . , he said . . .

                          Beam and rosin

      a seasonless swimming light   *o,*

Maybe I'll be a star   shrugged the earth

The sun would be everywhere in any case   blood orange the ladders

                in orbit

THE EARTH BLOOMS IN WITH AFFECTIONATE EMPTINESS

The scars of the sun are turning to honey. Lustrous recovery. Bee of the cairn.

Loose little fists of ranunculous and bees.

*

Rose belongs to lotus.

Lotus belongs to drone and queen.

*

Two suns rose and the birds flew down.   Loose little fists in the sea.

New planet of Pripyat and a taste of tin.

*

The bee

is a low yellow cloud coming out of a dream of dark scarves.

*

There, the cameo of the tiger horse.

*

Pear. Rosemary and pear.

*

Loose little fists of apples and the moon.

*

Daybreak is an emergency of twelve thousand larks.

Sky without heaven.   Blushing honey.

Theater of the heartbeat.   Loose little fists.

*

*

Be born.

Be born from the cloud with its door. The cloud from the sea where the birds

are suddenly swimming.

LATE VALENTINE

in the bed of lakes, buried valentines

apricots from the tree

dogstar hobbles

midnight bends

listen earthfruit

murmur in

MONSTER/UNBECOMING

Wear the Cassini tie. Its peach waves and unreal flowers.   Green to be gladly overlaid

by a darker leaf

poison in the speech   come in become

sweet.   Nose the lilies sung by the sun from underneath

There: an iridescent hare   Stay still

in the black field   my name is not

To be gladly   by the darker green   the sting

the phrase of your seeing

Who with their ladling beaks emptied the sea

the birds
Dear B,

Against the roof of new earth the   forest seahorse   resists its birth

the lily its equal   in illegible hindsight

I do not know how to tell you:

garden of lilies, the dead horse   I had been raised to read

in a small gold crown   I had dogs and not a staff

birds in the dogbane in the bed of leaves lay down

The teal earth yields nothing, but.   Iris   iris   oak

Islands drift off of you   Floating oaks   their scripts surface in twilight.

I admit that I read Antares, and you in it.   Near kestrel.   Raptor   Fault line.

The light a perfume of opera   & port. It shines all over you.

*

The tree   leafless   gave off too gradual

its light.

*

There, the bodiless hand stirs the stream. Black it out.

*

How many stories the sundown?

The lids of my tobacco tins are singing all over you.   Dark Blue Tiger.

*

I step into myself and out, eyes everywhere.   Blackberry and apple in the pondweed.

Nonetheless, nothing stays. Not the blackness   not the winter

of your terrible hands.   Violent diva   God is also a boxer

out of the ring.   Glasses break in the landlocked town.

A fish hears them and forgets.

Later it is eating a school of fish and is reminded.

One among them tastes iridescent   a lemon and an octopus mating in its mouth.

Furrow of God   It does not end, or begin   The book of your hands unsettled

(the dragons

There, the unsolvable sorrow of mountains

Where the stem meets the leaf
(my own private branch)

Where the stem meets the leaf God's dementia but the path of it directed   a Patient Red Tree.

God was none of those things but a green leaf on an upturned bucket the same shade of green.

*

earth   and seismograph

*

In one hand a pulse   in another its echo

forgery   resuscitation

NURSING HOME SUBLIME

MUTE SWAN

It was a white bird with a bear's body   :   white hibernator.   Seeker

of consolations   The wing cave

Draft-voice   a consolation.

*

There were no dry rivers. Only rivers more blue, rivers more brown.

Electricity ran under the roots and around them.

On the melting surface a thousand sweet onions.

The ice a permanent light.

The bear's wide collar of wings

the black beak a loose secondhand of the sky.

*

The melting impermanent light and the animals, yellow coats with black buttons.

*

Magnolia blossom, do not rust shut over the swan boat.   Styrofoam cups

shuffle under the seats   the gossip of moons.

WINTER

Beauty, bite your tongue there are flamingos   the blood of frost   flamingos

my eyes

among apples

obsidian

Mars beads   What is breathing

not the oars not the rower   (not usually)

There are things that live through time,

and resemble us.

Straightjacket of rubies   the boat

that breathes

Vascular in the plaid hour   lake anenome   lace

                    cumulus

                                        Epic flower

                                              Famous spider

                    nursing white air

NIGHT BLOOMING

Blueprint and approximate, your hand

A ghost with not finding

Wanderer to the fathom

Lost circles

— approximate retreat of the lie —

A door without a frame

TUNDRA

where I met you

in a tussle of spores

I would like to taste your

*

*

*

Caught in the middle in

humming larch   grid of the missing center

measuring the exit of winter

undead in the den

you are, and underneath the sea the sea thistle, and far-off, and between us

a score of arches.

Lower the softly clutching bodies into their visible.

The white garden is catching nests

A BONELESS BIRD

The truth a shortcut through your closet door.

Your going soul a honeycomb. I asked and asking

a ghost and no answer. Clues

the purring downlife

and cherries hummingbirds become.

Borrowed the flutter and I

to the empty hall. Window I said

to the window in the empty hall: Something

something. I to the going steadfast

unfastened

SHARIRA

Forever the black daffodil and then a laughing emptiness made several

in the Italian factory.

The painters have stolen an egg and one soccer ball and another egg was crushed.

Invitation and distance to *the expected obedience of your thoughts.*

A green sun rises. The green sun turns tenderly

in its harness to shine on the broken bill of the goose and then equally

on its unbroken companion

LIGHT GREEN LEAVES

Clairvoyance of the living body   concentration   *sharira*   harbor of marrow

the wandering pole   an animal of water   at a distance

the speech ponds   the eyed trees   & trees of reindeer   cranes of lace tree

in the city   of sea the sea woods   Once this sky was the ice floe of foxes

*

Something plain in the air

The sun   coming out of the dust   the desire path traveled in

Shoulder out the boulder of water   the love that says nothing saying more

Name her November

for her gold shouldering of white shadows

*

Mountain glacier

at the snow line   Snowflake the better flower   Faith the better statue

*

The desire path, also known as a desire line, is a path developed by erosion caused by animal or human footfall. The path usually represents the shortest or most easily navigated route between an origin and destination. The width and amount of erosion of the line represents the amount of demand. In Finland, planners are known to visit parks immediately after the first snowfall, when the existing paths are not visible, to see the first ones form.

I like to walk backwards in uneven circles   This is how I wander   Pleasure motility

*

Yin's Water presence, and stillness, deeper than the Blood's repose   Light green leaves

Kidney Water Exhausted a condition of Empty Fire   Light green leaves

The Water cannot embrace the Fire   Light green leaves

the Fire flutters inappropriately   Light green leaves

Weak Life Gate Fire   Light green leaves

*

We look at the sun. (Look at the sun with me). Our eyes sense something bright.

Sintered wind crusts Sun crusts   firn mirrors

Sun crusts form due to solar melting and refreezing. A specific type of crust called firn mirror causes the rare but spectacular reflection referred to as glacier fire. The mirror surface is transparent and acts as a greenhouse. Liquid and warmed water is present under the surface. Snow algae thrive under the protective surface of the mirror.

Hail and spatial dendrite

*

Space is filled with frozen water. The nucleus of a comet is a loosely compacted lump of ice.

In the sea-girt hemisphere at the door of the Sun, royal jelly in our throats.

APPENDIX

Gratitude is due many people in variably traceable ways. An inadequate list includes:

Frequent conversations with visual artist and dear friend Heide Hinrichs, which often include sharing works-in-progress, especially inform these poems; I have no record of how, except in the cases where I include the titles of her shows or pieces, *The expected obedience of your thoughts*, *Rose belongs to lotus*, and *The stars withdraw from the sky*. This last is a variation of Emily Dickinson's "the clouds withdrew from the sky."

"Autobiography" was under the influence of the films of Chris Marker, particularly *Grin Without a Cat*. The poem also owes a great deal to the subtitles from Alain Resnais' *Hiroshima, Mon Amour* and Jean Rouche's *Chronicle of a Summer*, as well as the structure of Sei Shonagon's *Pillow Book*.

"Winter" was inspired by Richard Weibe's beautiful short film *Aliki*.

"Night Blooming" lives in the shadow of Robert Rauschenberg's lost paintings by the same name.

"Tract" owes twice to poet Rob Schlegel. First for inviting me to write a poem to Lake Erie, and then for sharing his father's travel notes with me, from which "port of morrow" (I think this is on a road sign somewhere between Missoula and Portland) is lifted.

The films of Russian animator Yuri Norstein are the reason "Tango of the Tired Sun" and "Late Valentine" exist.

Garden of lilies, the dead horse is from Cecília Meireles's poem "The Dead Horse," translated by James Merrill.

A variation of "Light Green Leaves" exists as "Speech Ponds," a drawing animation and poem made with visual artist Kate Parry and musician and writer Thomas Fox Parry. Much of what happens in that poem is borrowed from textbooks I no longer have about the chemistry of ice and snow, as well as *The Web That Has No Weaver* by Ted Kaptchuk, and the Wikipedia entry on the desire path. "Light Green Leaves" was the title of a song by Little Wings long before it was the title of my poem.

"The Earth Blooms in with Affectionate Emptiness" had another life on vinyl as *Felt*, a sound installation created with musician Gust Burns for a residency at Seattle's Jack Straw New Media Gallery.

*"Monster/*Unbecoming" had a life as an artist book and performance thanks to the rhythmic leaf drawings of visual artist Blake Bronson-Bartlett.

My own private branch is from Bjork's song "Unison."

The deed is airless and weightless is something the lovely artist Gretchen Bennett said to describe the poignance of Proposition Joe's death in *The Wire*.

"A Boneless Bird" is for Paula Jones Gardiner. It appears elsewhere as "Song."

ACKNOWLEDGMENTS

Thanks to the following journals and anthologies where these poems first appeared:

"Tract" in *LVNG*

"The Lion Ant" and "Strangel Mine" in *The Arcadia Project*

"Autobiography" in *Weekday*

"Warm Earth" in *Anomalous*

"Winter" in *Mare Nostrum*

"Light Green Leaves" as "Speech Ponds" in *The Volta*

I wish to thank the editors of these publications, as well as my family, teachers and friends, particularly Don Mee Choi, Alejandro de Acosta, Cristin Miller, Elizabeth Robinson, Cole Swensen, and Karena Youtz, for their care and close readings, and Martha Sutton, Ray and Patricia Noel, and Heather Noel-Acar for their generous support. Deepest thanks too to Lori Anderson Moseman and Matthew Klane for their patience and humor. To all of the kind people and works of art in the Appendix, I would like to extend my deepest thanks. Love and gratitude to Bob Gronhovd for the use of his painting, *G.O.G.*, which informs *The Monarchs'* cover, created by Heide Hinrichs. For her interpretation, vision, labor and friendship, the author is very grateful. Finally, sincerest thanks to Helen Berggruen, Hilary Rand, Tulsa, and Simone, for the August of verbena, ichor, and oak. Thanks also go to Cosmo.

BIOGRAPHICAL NOTE

Melanie Noel grew up in Oregon and lives in Seattle, Washington, where she is a gardener and teaches workshops on synesthesia and imagination in parks, schools, and community centers. Her poems have appeared in *Weekday*, *LVNG*, *The Volta* and *The Arcadia Project*. She's also written poems for short films and installations, and co-curated APOSTROPHE, a dance, music, and poetry series, with musician Gust Burns and dancers Michèle Steinwald and Beth Graczyk.

MEANDER SCAR Series

In the aftermath of Federal Disaster #1649, a flood along the Delaware River, Lori Anderson Moseman and Tom Moseman created the press Stockport Flats to celebrate writers and artists whose creative buoyancy builds community. This series, *Meander Scar*, features wordsmiths who carve new pathways. The geological term, *flood meander scar*, refers to a river's "experimentation" as high water forges new flow patterns. Post-flood, the mainstream may never frequent these pathways; however, the record of such possibilities intensifies our awareness of how terrain changes. *Meander* conjures whimsy; *scar* suggests both injury and healing. Let's examine forms that enact such fullness.

Designed by Lori Anderson Moseman, this volume was created using Hoefler Text and Century Gothic, printed on 80 lb paper by BookMobile. Jacket design is by Heide Hinrichs. This on-demand edition has an initial printing of 200 copies.

MEANDER SCAR Titles

B_____ Meditations [1-52] by Matthew Klane (2008)
Building Codes by Belle Gironda (2009)
Elements by Deborah Poe (2010)
The Spectra by Fred Muratori (2011)
How We Saved the City by Kate Schapira (2012)
poem for the house by Katie Yates (2012)
The Monarchs by Melanie Noel (2013)
Decoherence by Belinda Kremer (2013)

Stockport **Flats** 2013

1120 East Martin Luther King Jr. Street   Ithaca, NY 14850   (607) 272-1630

www.stockportflats.org